P9-CFS-357

RAIN FOREST ECOSYSTEMS

by Tammy Gagne

Content Consultant
James S. Godde
McGrath Professor of Biology
Monmouth College

Core Library

An Imprint of Abdo Publishing
abdopublishing.com

abdopublishing.com

Published by Abdo Publishing, a division of ABDO, PO Box 398166, Minneapolis, Minnesota 55439. Copyright © 2016 by Abdo Consulting Group, Inc. International copyrights reserved in all countries. No part of this book may be reproduced in any form without written permission from the publisher. Core Library™ is a trademark and logo of Abdo Publishing.

Printed in the United States of America, North Mankato, Minnesota
022015
092015

Cover Photo: Roberto A. Sanchez/iStockphoto
Interior Photos: Roberto A. Sanchez/iStockphoto, 1; iStockphoto, 4, 17; Shutterstock Images, 7, 15, 18, 21, 24, 28 (background), 28 (center), 28 (middle right), 28 (bottom right), 28 (bottom left), 30, 45; Rich Carey/Shutterstock Images, 9; Dr. Morley Read/ Shutterstock Images, 12; Ksenia Ragozina/Shutterstock Images, 22; Tami Freed/ Shutterstock Images, 28 (top left); Tristan Tan/Shutterstock Images, 28 (top right); Fabio Pupin/Visuals Unlimited/Corbis, 34; Lee Prince/Shutterstock Images, 36; John Van Hasselt/Corbis, 39; Eduardo Verdugo/AP Images, 40; Natalia Bratslavsky/Shutterstock Images, 43

Editor: Arnold Ringstad
Series Designer: Becky Daum

Library of Congress Control Number: 2015931043

Cataloging-in-Publication Data
Gagne, Tammy.
 Rain forest ecosystems / Tammy Gagne.
   p. cm. -- (Ecosystems of the world)
Includes bibliographical references and index.
ISBN 978-1-62403-856-3
1. Rain forest ecology--Juvenile literature. 2. Rain forests--Juvenile literature. 3. Rain forest conservation--Juvenile literature.   I. Title.
577.34--dc23
                                    2015931043

CONTENTS

CHAPTER ONE

WHAT IS A RAIN FOREST?

The spider monkey zipped through the treetops. The tiny creature searched for water. The air in the Amazon Rain Forest was hot and humid. The active animal needed a drink.

Fortunately for the spider monkey, water was always nearby. The monkey had seen some dripping leaves earlier. As the animal moved toward the water, it stepped on what looked like a branch covered in

Spider monkeys are found in the tropical rain forests of South America and Central America.

moss. Then the branch started to move. It turned out to be a sloth. This type of animal sometimes moves so slowly that moss grows on it.

By the time the spider monkey reached the water, a huge spider had already found it. A goliath tarantula was quenching its own thirst. The monkey backed away from the hairy creature. It would wait until the tarantula was finished. Life in the rain forest was never boring.

A Damp Ecosystem

Rain forests are dense jungles filled with tall trees. They receive much more rainfall than other forests. Tropical rain forests can get up to 400 inches (1,000 cm) of rain each year. These wet environments are ideal for certain types of wildlife. Many of these species are only found in rain forests. Rain forests cover only about 6 percent of Earth's surface. But they are home to more than half of the world's plant and animal species.

Frequent, heavy rains make rain forests very damp places.

These organisms and their environment make up the rain forest's ecosystems. Everything in an ecosystem—even the soil and water—affects everything else. Animals eat plants or each other. Plants and animals both need soil and water.

Ecosystems Large and Small

A rain forest is a large ecosystem made up of many smaller ones. In the Amazon Rain Forest, the lowest areas make up the floodplain. The land closest to the rivers is known as the *váreza*. The terra firma ecosystem lies away from the rivers. And the *igapó* is the forest that lines the blackwater rivers of the region. Each of these areas is its own unique ecosystem. Each plays a part in the larger ecosystem of the Amazon.

Rain Forests at Risk

If just one plant or animal disappears, it can have a wide impact on other organisms. A complex web of predators, prey, and plants connects the rain forest ecosystems.

These ecosystems face many threats. Logging, farming, and mining chip away at them. At one time rain forests were twice as

Rain forests around the world are being cleared to make way for farms.

The Four Layers

Rain forests are made up of four basic layers. The highest is the emergent layer. Many trees in this section measure 200 feet (60 m) tall. Animals living in the emergent layer include birds, butterflies, and spider monkeys. Just below the emergent layer lies the canopy. It is home to animals such as birds, frogs, and snakes. Many of these animals spend their entire lives in the canopy, never touching the ground. The understory layer lies below the canopy. It is heavily shaded. Plants growing in the understory have large leaves to collect as much sunlight as possible. Only the forest floor is lower and darker than the understory. Very few plants can survive in an area with so little sunlight. But some animal species, such as anteaters, thrive there.

large as they are today. Scientists predict the rain forests could disappear completely within the next 100 years. Many people are taking action to stop this from happening.

British explorer Ed Stafford has seen firsthand how much wildlife exists in the rain forests. In 2010 he became the first person to walk from one end of the Amazon River to the other. His journey took 859 days. He described the trek in a magazine article:

> I wanted to create an adventure so exciting that it would spark interest in an area that many people have no direct connection with.
>
> We spent a lot of our time walking through flooded forest. Sometimes, we walked chest deep in brown water. We encountered electric eels almost 7 feet [2.1m] long, able to knock a person unconscious with the electric shock that they deliver. We bathed in rivers full of caiman crocodiles. At first, we were cautious, but after a few months, we realized that the caimans were very timid and would not bother us. When food was scarce, I sometimes ate piranha fish and tortoises.

Source: Gail Skroback Hennessey. "A Long, Hot Walk." Appleseeds January, 2012: 10–11. Print. 10.

Changing Minds

Imagine you are taking part in a debate at school. Your teacher has asked you to argue whether Stafford should have gone into the rain forest. How might you use the information above to support your point?

CHAPTER TWO

HOT AND HUMID

Most rain forests are located near the equator. These are called tropical rain forests. They remain warm all year long. The temperature in a tropical rain forest rarely goes below 68 degrees Fahrenheit (20°C). The forests often reach temperatures as high as 93 degrees Fahrenheit (34°C).

A smaller number of rain forests exist far north and south of the equator. These cooler regions are

The Amazon Rain Forest is one of the world's most famous tropical rain forests.

known as temperate rain forests. Their temperatures vary more than those found in tropical rain forests. In the winter, temperatures can fall almost to the freezing mark, 32 degrees Fahrenheit (0°C).

Summertime temperatures can climb to 80 degrees Fahrenheit (27°C). But the average temperature stays between 39 and 54 degrees Fahrenheit (4–12°C).

Temperate rain forests receive less rain than tropical rain forests. They may get as little as 60 inches (152 cm) or as much as 200 inches (508 cm) each year.

Alaskan Rain Forest

Some people are surprised to learn rain forests are not just found in the tropics. They exist throughout the world, even in Alaska. The Tongass National Forest in Southeast Alaska is a temperate rain forest. Its wildlife ranges from the tiny red squirrel to the massive moose. The lush environment is filled with ferns, mosses, and other plants.

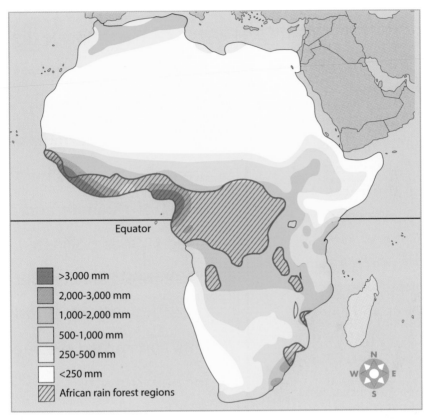

Rain in African Rain Forests

This map shows the rain forests of Africa. It also shows the average annual rainfall for the continent. How does being near the equator seem to affect rainfall?

Legend:
- >3,000 mm
- 2,000-3,000 mm
- 1,000-2,000 mm
- 500-1,000 mm
- 250-500 mm
- <250 mm
- African rain forest regions

Equator

Each Species Is Important

The rains in tropical rain forests create a perfect environment for many types of wildlife. Each species plays a special role in rain forest ecosystems. Many species depend on one another for their survival.

Rising Temperatures

A major threat to the rain forests is global warming. The Earth's average temperature is increasing. This is caused by too much carbon dioxide in the atmosphere. As temperatures rise, the rain forests' climates change. This can harm plants and animals that have evolved to survive in a particular climate. Rain forests are an important defense against climate change. Plants and trees in the rain forests take in carbon dioxide and give off oxygen. By protecting the rain forests, people can help slow the increase of carbon dioxide in the atmosphere.

One example is the Brazil nut tree. It thrives in the moist conditions of the Amazon's terra firma areas. But it needs help from both animals and insects. Bees pollinate these trees. Small rodents called agoutis eat Brazil nuts and spread the seeds for new growth.

The Brazil nut tree can grow to more than 150 feet (46 m) tall.

PLANTS OF THE RAIN FOREST

The Amazon Rain Forest is home to more than 80,000 different plant species. As many as 100 different types of trees can live within a few minutes' walk of each other. Rain forests provide an ideal environment for many plants and trees. Vines and palms grow easily in this moist setting.

Vines twist and turn through the forests. Some rain forest animals eat these plants. People use

Palms are among the most common trees in the Amazon Rain Forest.

them for making food, medicine, and construction materials. Vines also serve as paths for small animals and insects.

Palms are used throughout the world. The leaves of these plants can be made into brooms, hammocks, and even necklaces. Some palm species produce oil. Many everyday products in grocery stores contain palm oil. It can be found in foods, cosmetics, and cleaners.

Epiphytes and Bromeliads

Some kinds of plants do not get their nutrients from the soil. Instead they get them from the air or from water. They are known as epiphytes. These plants sometimes

Armed and Dangerous

Certain animals can defend themselves against predators. Plants can protect themselves too. Some plants simply taste terrible. Animals learn to avoid eating them. Others have rough edges that make them hard to eat. Many rain forest plants, such as the cashew tree, produce toxins. These poisonous chemicals will sicken animals that eat the plant.

Palm trees used to harvest palm oil are grown in vast plantations.

grow on top of other plants. Up to one quarter of the plant species in lowland rain forest areas are epiphytes. They include certain types of ferns, mosses, and orchids.

Some epiphytes are also bromeliads. These plants have leaves shaped like cups that hold rainwater. The

Bromeliads store water within their overlapping leaves.

plants collect moisture from the damp rain forest air. The best-known bromeliad is the pineapple plant.

The leaves of bromeliads are like tiny ecosystems. The algae growing inside them feed various insects. Some crabs, salamanders, and worms can spend their entire lives within a bromeliad. Bromeliads help animal species survive by providing them with water. Small animals such as snails and tree frogs rely on them to survive.

EXPLORE ONLINE

Chapter Three discusses plants known as bromeliads. The website below includes more information about these water-storing plants. As you know, every source is different. How are bromeliads presented differently in this chapter and on the website? Does the website support what you have read in the chapter? Did you learn any new information?

Bromeliads of the Rain Forest
mycorelibrary.com/rain-forest-ecosystems

CHAPTER FOUR

ANIMALS OF THE RAIN FOREST

The animals that live in the world's rain forests are as diverse as the plants that live there. Hundreds of different bird species can live within just a few square miles of rain forest. Some rain forest birds are large, such as the scarlet macaw. Other birds are tiny, such as the black-breasted puffleg. This species is an extremely rare hummingbird. Big or small, each animal plays an important part in the rain forest ecosystem.

Scarlet macaws are among the most colorful rain forest animals.

A Balancing Act

A change in the population of one animal species can have an effect on many others. The jaguar offers an example of this. As jaguars have become endangered, the animals they eat have grown in numbers. Snake populations may increase. These additional snakes eat more birds, decreasing the bird population. The insects the birds normally eat may grow in numbers because there are fewer birds to eat them. This change can have a damaging effect on the plants the insects eat. Small changes can ripple through the rain forest ecosystem.

Working Animals

In the rain forest, birds and bats perform the important job of pollination, carrying pollen from plant to plant. This process makes it possible for plants to reproduce. In the rain forests of Panama, birds pollinate more than 40 percent of plants.

The organisms involved in the process are adapted to their roles. Birds use their beaks to drink the watery nectar of bright-colored flowers. Bats are drawn to thicker nectar. This nectar is found in flowers that only open at night, when the bats are active.

Insects also pollinate plants. Bees' preferred flowers open during the day and offer places for them to sit as they collect nectar. Even beetles and flies take part in pollination. Flowers draw these insects with their appealing scents.

Eating to Live

Animals help some plants of the rain forest by eating them. Animals of all sizes play a part. From the tiny tree shrew to the gigantic elephant, many rain forest animals eat figs. Often these animals avoid eating the seeds, instead discarding them on the ground. Other animals eat the seeds and leave them behind in their waste. In both cases the seeds

Endangered Animals

Over time human beings have destroyed about half of the world's rain forests. As a result, many animals are now endangered species. This means they are at risk of dying out. Scientists estimate about 15 percent of the animals that once lived in the rain forests have become extinct. If humans continue to destroy Earth's rain forests, these ecosystems may be changed forever.

A Rain Forest Food Web

In this diagram, lines between the organisms show how energy moves through the web. Energy from the sun helps plants grow. Some animals eat the plants for energy, while others eat other animals. Worms feed on dead animals and plants. Think of another species you have read about. How might it fit into this food web? How might it connect to other organisms?

are scattered in new areas, where they grow into more fig trees.

A Connected Ecosystem

Energy in rain forest ecosystems comes from the sun. Its light helps plants grow. When an animal eats a plant, it uses that energy to survive. When this animal becomes prey for another animal, the predator takes in this energy. The energy passes from link to link in a food chain. The chain goes from tiny plants all the way up to the top predators in an ecosystem.

A single ecosystem may have many food chains. When these chains connect together, the result is known as a food web. Food webs show how energy moves around in an ecosystem. Each species in the web relies on other species for the energy it needs to survive.

CHAPTER FIVE

PEOPLE AND THE RAIN FORESTS

Plants and animals are not the only living beings that play major roles in the rain forests. People also affect these ecosystems. Some people live in or near the rain forests. Many of them depend on the land for their livelihood. Other people live far from the rain forests. Their actions also can have a significant effect on these ecosystems.

People who live near rain forests often use the forests' resources to survive.

Leaving Some for Later

Rain forests produce many of the raw materials used in manufacturing. Pulp is used for paper, rubber is used in automobile tires, and wax is used for plastics. All of these resources are found in tropical rain forests. The plants and trees that produce these items are renewable resources. This means rain forests can grow more pulp, rubber, and wax. But it is important to harvest only a reasonable amount of these resources. If too much is taken too quickly, the rain forests may not be able to keep up.

Living Off the Rain Forests

More than half of the world's rain forests are located in countries suffering from severe poverty. The people of these nations turn to farming, ranching, and logging to support their families. Problems arise when too much land is taken for this purpose.

As the human population rises, more food is needed. Farming in and near the rain forests helps put food on people's tables. But it does more than just that. Plants grown in rain forests are used in many non-food products, including lipstick and fuel. Products from the rain forest have become a big business. However, once rain forest land is taken away, it is almost never regrown. It is reused for other purposes. With the rain forests shrinking, many plants and animals are suffering.

Rain Forest Threats

In some cases national governments have created laws to protect endangered animals and plants. In Indonesia, for example, it is illegal to hunt Sumatran tigers. However, many poachers continue to kill these endangered animals. The tigers can be sold for up to $5,000 each. Poachers sell the tigers' body parts for use in ancient Chinese medicines.

Indonesia has put limits on logging to save its rain forests. Today most of the deforestation in the country is from illegal logging. Laws to protect rain forests will only help if they are enforced. The large profits available from selling rain forest products continue to drive people to poach and log illegally.

People living far from the rain forests can also
harm these ecosystems. Pollution from factories
around the world adds to the problem of global
warming. Even shoppers play a role in helping or
hurting the rain forests. People make buying decisions
every day. Choosing to buy certain items can affect
the demand for natural resources taken from rain
forests. People can make a difference when they reuse
or recycle an item instead of buying a new one.

Some researchers think certain types of rain forest plants could be used to treat cancer. *Ottawa Citizen* journalist Stuart Grudgings writes:

> *In a jungle so dense it all but blocks out the sun, [a] 46-year-old [man] shimmies up a thin tree helped by a harness, a strap between his feet, and the expertise gained from a lifetime labouring in the forest. A few well-placed snips later, branches cascade to a small band of researchers and a doctor—who faithfully make a long monthly trip to the Cuieiras river in Amazonas state in the belief that the forest's staggeringly rich plant life can unlock new treatments for cancer. They may be right. About 70 percent of current cancer drugs are either natural products or derived from natural compounds, and the world's largest rain forest is a great cauldron of biodiversity that has already produced medicine for diseases such as malaria.*

> Source: Stuart Grudgings. "Fighting for life in the Amazon." The Ottawa Citizen. The Ottawa Citizen. November 18, 2009. Web. Accessed October 26, 2014.

What's the Big Idea?

Take a closer look at the above passage. What is the journalist's main idea? What evidence does he offer to support this point?

CHAPTER SIX

THE FUTURE OF THE RAIN FORESTS

No one knows exactly what the future holds for the rain forests. If people continue to harvest their natural resources, the rain forests could suffer greatly. Much depends on the steps people take now to protect these important ecosystems.

One of the biggest problems facing the rain forests today is soil erosion. The trees that grow in rain forests help anchor the soil to the forest floor.

Many rain forests, including Alaska's Tongass National Forest, are protected by governments.

As more trees are cut down, heavy rains wash away the soil in many places. Without soil, many plants cannot keep growing.

Excessive farming is making this problem worse. Many crops, such as coffee and tobacco, harm the topsoil when they are planted. If given a break between crops, the soil can recover. But farmers often plant one crop right after another on the same land. This can make the soil unusable. Farmers replace their lost land by taking over more rain forest.

New Discoveries Await

Scientists think there could be as many as 30,000 undiscovered plants. Many of the species are likely growing in the rain forests. Learning about these plants could help us find cures for deadly illnesses. It could even inspire more people to help save the rain forests. The future of our planet may depend on the future of these vital ecosystems.

What We Can Do

The countries of the United Nations (UN) are working to save the rain forests by stopping deforestation. The UN realizes the goal cannot

Countries around the world are working together to stop deforestation.

39

National and business leaders are taking steps to save Earth's rain forests.

be accomplished overnight. For this reason, its plan calls for gradual changes. The first goal is to reduce deforestation by 50 percent by 2020. The UN then hopes to end deforestation altogether by 2030.

Some important nations are not taking part in this plan. Two of the largest carbon-producing countries in the world are China and India. Neither of these nations has agreed to take part. It is not too late, however. Nations can join in the organized effort at a later date.

People everywhere can make changes to help the rain forests. They can recycle as many items as possible instead of buying new products. They can spread the word about the world's rain forests. Raising awareness is an important step toward finding solutions.

FURTHER EVIDENCE

Chapter Six covers the future of rain forests and discusses efforts to save them. What was one of the main points of this chapter? What evidence is included to support this point? Read the article at the website below. Does the information on the website support the main point of the chapter? Does it present new evidence?

Saving the Rain Forests

mycorelibrary.com/rain-forest-ecosystems

WELL-KNOWN RAIN FORESTS

Amazon Rain Forest

Located in South America, the Amazon Rain Forest is the largest tropical rain forest in the world. It is home to 40,000 plant species, 1,300 bird species, 3,000 types of fish, 430 mammal species, and 2.5 million types of insects.

Congo Rain Forest

The Congo Rain Forest is the world's second-largest tropical rain forest. It is located in central Africa. Many exotic animals live in the Congo, including apes, elephants, and 700 different species of river fish.

Daintree Rain Forest

The Daintree Rain Forest is found in Australia. This rain forest is home to some incredibly rare species. Animals that live in the Daintree Rain Forest include the white-lipped tree frog, the Ulysses butterfly, and the Bennett's tree-kangaroo.

Elk are among the animals that roam in the rain forest of Olympic National Park.

Olympic National Park

Located in the northwestern United States, Olympic National Park is a temperate rain forest. The air is cooler here than in tropical rain forests, but the humid environment is ideal for many plant species. Lush green trees topped with moss and dense ferns are found throughout the park.

Dig Deeper

After reading this book, what questions do you still have about rain forests? Do you want to learn more about a specific plant or animal? Write down one or two questions to guide your research. With an adult's help, find a few reliable sources that can help answer your questions. Write a few sentences about how you did your research and what you learned from it.

Why Do I Care?

Chances are good you live far away from a rain forest. Why should you care if these ecosystems thrive or struggle to survive? Search online to find out the kinds of items that come from rain forest resources. Do you use any of these items? Write a few sentences about what you learn.

Say What?

Studying rain forests can mean learning a lot of new vocabulary. Find five words in this book that you have never heard before. Use a dictionary to find out what they mean. Then write the meanings in your own words, and use each word in a new sentence.

Tell the Tale

Chapter One of this book discusses an explorer's experience hiking along the Amazon River in South America. Imagine you are making a similar journey in a rain forest. Write 200 words about the animals and plants you encounter on your trip. How could you avoid harming the ecosystem?

GLOSSARY

blackwater river
a deep, slow-moving river that is dark in color

bromeliad
tropical plants with long, stiff leaves that collect rainwater

deforestation
the act or process of clearing forests by cutting down trees

ecosystem
a community of living things interacting with their environment

epiphyte
a plant that gets moisture and nutrients from the air

erosion
the process of being worked away through the movement of water, wind, or glacial ice

extinct
no longer existing

poacher
a person who hunts illegally

pollinate
to move pollen within or between plants

temperate
having a mild climate

topsoil
surface soil, usually including the rich upper layer where plants have most of their roots

LEARN MORE

Books

Aloian, Molly, and Bobby Kalman. *A Rain Forest Habitat*. Washington, DC: National Geographic School Publications, 2010.

Eye Wonder: Rain Forest. New York: DK Publishing, 2013.

Stewart, Melissa, and Allen Young. *No Monkeys, No Chocolate*. Watertown, MA: Charlesbridge Publishing, 2013.

Websites

To learn more about Ecosystems of the World, visit **booklinks.abdopublishing.com**. These links are routinely monitored and updated to provide the most current information available.

Visit **mycorelibrary.com** for free additional tools for teachers and students.

INDEX

ABOUT THE AUTHOR

Tammy Gagne has written more than 100 books for adults and children. She resides in northern New England with her husband and son. One of her favorite pastimes is visiting schools to talk to children about the writing process.